THIS BOOK BELONGS TO

. . . .

MY AWESOME BROTHER

My Awesome Brother
A book about transgender acceptance

Published in Australia by
MABEL Media
Postal: Post Office Box 246, Castlemaine 3450
Email: lisefrances.books@gmail.com
Website: www.lisefrances.com.au

First published in Australia 2019
Copyright © Lisé Frances 2019

National Library of Australia Cataloguing – in – Publication entry

 A catalogue record for this book is available from the National Library of Australia

ISBN 978-0-6483676-5-9
Cover, layout, design and illustrations by Karina Parra, karixen@gmail.com
Printed by Kindle Direct Publishing

All rights reserved. No part of this publication may be reproduced, stored in a retrieval system, or transmitted, in any form or by any means without the prior written permission of the publisher, nor be otherwise circulated in any form of binding or cover other than that in which it is published and without a similar condition being imposed on the subsequent purchaser.

All contact details given in this book were current at the time of publication, but are subject to change.

MY AWESOME BROTHER

A book about transgender acceptance

By Lisé Frances

My big sister Donna wasn't happy.
So I tried to make her happy by doing silly stuff.
I tried something different each day.

On Sunday I pretended to be a dog. I crawled around and woofed, and sat up and begged, and made sad puppy eyes... But that didn't work.

On Monday I pulled really funny faces and crossed my eyes and made weird noises...
But that didn't work.

On Tuesday I pretended to be a fabulous dancer and twirled and jumped and tippy toed all around the house...
But that didn't work.

On Wednesday I raided the dress up box and made myself look like a fairy clown ghost, and followed Donna all around the house making fairy clown ghost noises...
But that didn't work.

On Friday I put on my unicorn onesie and painted my face and did my hair all crazy.
But that didn't work either.

On Saturday I ran out of ideas, and I was sad too.

Then I found out why my big sister Donna had been sad. Donna wanted to be my big brother Jon. I like the name Jon.

Now I have a big brother, Jon. And Jon is heaps happier.
You know how I can tell?

Because Jon pulls funny faces with me and we laugh lots!

Because Jon dances and twirls and tippy toes all over the house with me and we laugh lots.

Because Jon raids the dress up box with me and we dress up as all sorts of things like fairies and clowns and robots, and we laugh lots.

Because Jon plays hide and seek with me and sometimes I win and sometimes Jon wins, and we laugh lots.

Because we paint our faces and do our hair all silly and we laugh and laugh and laugh!

I reckon my big brother Jon is awesome.

Lisé Frances loves our beautiful planet and the people on it. At heart she's a proud, tree-hugging hippy. She looks forward to equality for all people regardless of their colour, shape, size, or gender preference. Lisé believes the world would be boring without its brilliant and ever-changing diversity and underpins her writing with that mindset.

Resources

There are many websites and organisations available in Australia today, some of these may be useful and include assorted information and options to access support:

- Support for under 18yrs https://www.minus18.org.au

- Support for those with a transgender/gender diverse child http://www.transcendsupport.com.au

- Information around gender diversity https://au.reachout.com

- Services for the transgender and gender diverse community https://gendercentre.org.au

- Support including online chat option https://qlife.org.au

- Parents looking for help http://www.genderhelpforparents.com.au

- 'Starter kit' for the transgender person https://www.trans101.org.au

- Gender neutral pronouns https://lifehacker.com/how-to-use-gender-neutral-pronouns-1821239054?IR=T

*Please note all above resources were current at the time of publication.

Made in the USA
Columbia, SC
29 July 2022